W9-BLA-268

COOL
MAKERSPACE
GADGETS & GIZMOS

CONSTRUCT IT!
ARCHITECTURE YOU CAN BUILD, BREAK, AND BUILD AGAIN

Jessie Alkire

Checkerboard
Library

An Imprint of Abdo Publishing
abdopublishing.com

abdopublishing.com

Published by Abdo Publishing, a division of ABDO, PO Box 398166, Minneapolis, Minnesota 55439. Copyright © 2018 by Abdo Consulting Group, Inc. International copyrights reserved in all countries. No part of this book may be reproduced in any form without written permission from the publisher. Checkerboard Library™ is a trademark and logo of Abdo Publishing.

Printed in the United States of America, North Mankato, Minnesota
102017
012018

THIS BOOK CONTAINS RECYCLED MATERIALS

Design: Sarah DeYoung, Mighty Media, Inc.
Production: Mighty Media, Inc.
Editor: Liz Salzmann
Cover Photographs: Mighty Media, Inc.; Shutterstock
Interior Photographs: Mighty Media, Inc.; Shutterstock

The following manufacturers/names appearing in this book are trademarks: Artist's Loft™, Craft Smart®, K'NEX, LEGO®, Norcom®

Publisher's Cataloging-in-Publication Data
Names: Alkire, Jessie, author.
Title: Construct it! architecture you can build, break, and build again / by Jessie Alkire.
Other titles: Architecture you can build, break, and build again
Description: Minneapolis, Minnesota : Abdo Publishing, 2018. I Series: Cool makerspace gadgets & gizmos I Includes online resources and index.
Identifiers: LCCN 2017944032 I ISBN 9781532112522 (lib.bdg.) I ISBN 9781614799948 (ebook)
Subjects: LCSH: Architecture--Juvenile literature. I Creative ability in science--Juvenile literature. I Handicraft--Juvenile literature. I Makerspaces--Juvenile literature.
Classification: DDC 720--dc23
LC record available at https://lccn.loc.gov/2017944032

TO ADULT HELPERS

This is your chance to assist a young maker as they develop new skills, gain confidence, and make cool things! These activities are designed to help children create projects in makerspaces. Children may need more assistance for some activities than others. Be there to offer guidance when they need it. Encourage them to do as much as they can on their own. Be a cheerleader for their creativity.

Before getting started, remember to lay down ground rules for using tools and supplies and for cleaning up. There should always be adult supervision when using a hot or sharp tool.

SAFETY SYMBOL

Some projects in this book require the use of sharp tools. That means you'll need some adult help for these projects. Determine whether you'll need help on a project by looking for this safety symbol.

SHARP!
This project requires the use of a sharp tool.

CONTENTS

What's a MAKERSPACE?

Think of a place humming with activity. Everywhere you look, people are designing and building awesome structures. Welcome to a makerspace!

Makerspaces are areas where people come together to create. They are the perfect places to design and build architecture projects! Makerspaces have all kinds of materials and tools. But a maker's best tool is his or her imagination. Makers invent new architecture projects. They also look at existing architecture projects and find ways to make them even cooler. Then, makers bring these projects to life! Are you ready to become a maker?

BEFORE YOU GET STARTED

GET PERMISSION

Ask an adult for **permission** to use the makerspace and materials before starting any project.

BE RESPECTFUL

Share tools and supplies with other makers. When you're done with a tool, put it back so others can use it.

MAKE A PLAN

Read through the instructions and gather all your supplies ahead of time.

BE CAREFUL

Some architecture pieces and tools are very small. Keep them organized as you create so they don't get lost!

WHAT IS ARCHITECTURE?

Architecture is the planning, designing, and constructing of buildings and other structures. People who do this job are called architects. Architecture is often considered an art form. Some buildings are famous for their architecture. Architects try to create structures that are both beautiful and strong. They also plan buildings that fit a specific purpose or use, such as government buildings, skyscrapers, or schools.

LEGOs

LEGOs are construction and architecture toys. They are plastic building blocks you can connect to build structures. There are many LEGO kits to make specific projects. Or, you can use the basic building blocks to create any structure you want! Many of the architecture projects in this book use LEGOs. You can buy LEGOs or similar building blocks in stores or **online**.

K'NEX

K'NEX are another type of architecture toy. They are made up of rods, connectors, gears, and wheels. You can use these parts to make all kinds of structures. K'NEX sells kits to make specific projects. It also sells basic sets that can be used to make anything you like! You can buy K'NEX in stores and online.

7

Here are some of the materials and tools used for the projects in this book. If your makerspace doesn't have what you need, don't worry! Find different supplies to substitute for the missing materials. Or modify the project to fit the supplies you have. Be creative!

birdseed

bouncy balls

cardboard box

colored pencils

craft knife

foam paintbrush

graph paper

K'NEX connectors

K'NEX rods

K'NEX 375 Piece Deluxe Building Set

LEGO axle plate

LEGO basic bricks

LEGO plates

measuring tape

CONSTRUCT IT! TECHNIQUES

paint

paper towel tube

DRAW IT OUT

Architects design and draw plans for structures they create. Use graph paper, a sketch pad, or plain paper to plan your architecture projects too. Draw in pencil so you can make changes if needed. If a design isn't working out, don't worry. Just flip to a new page and start again!

ATTACHING K'NEX

K'NEX clips, connectors, and rods come in a variety of sizes and styles. Practice attaching these pieces in different ways so you get used to how they fit together!

pencil

rubber bands

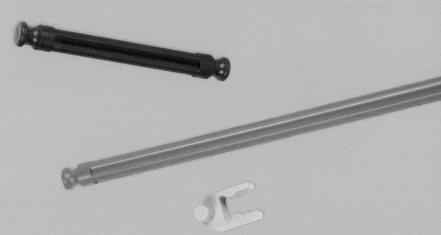

MODEL
BEDROOM

Use LEGOs to make a scale model of
your bedroom!

WHAT YOU NEED

measuring tape • paper
pencil • graph paper
ruler • colored pencils
large LEGO plate
LEGO basic bricks

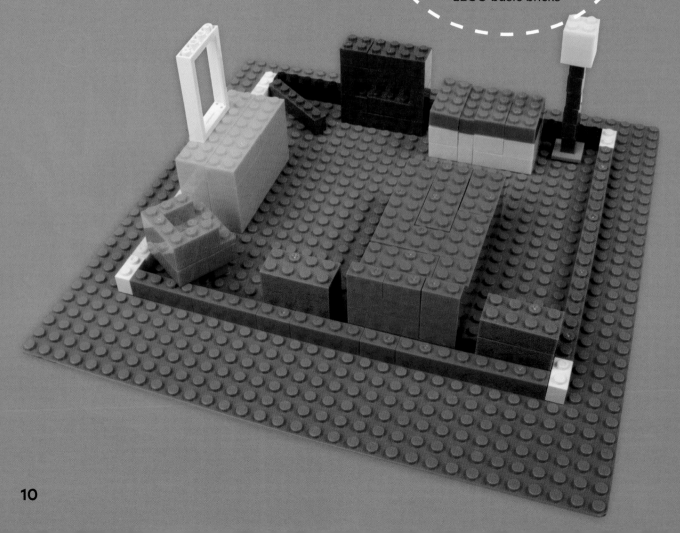

I. Measure the length and width of your bedroom. Measure the length, width, and height of each piece of furniture in your room. Write these measurements down.

2 Draw the outline of your room on graph paper. Two squares on the paper represent 1 foot (0.3 m) of your room measurements. So, if your room is 10 feet (3 m) wide, that would equal 20 squares on the paper.

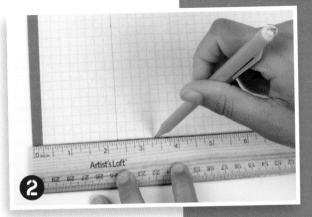

3 Use the measurements from step 1 to draw in your bedroom furniture. Color the furniture with colored pencils. The completed drawing is the plan for your LEGO model.

4 Use LEGO bricks to form the outline of your room on the LEGO plate. Each **stud** on the plate represents one square on your graph paper.

5. Use LEGO bricks to build models of your furniture inside the outline.

6. Compare your model to your real bedroom. How **accurate** did the model's spacing and setup turn out?

DOUBLE-DECKER BIRD FEEDER

Build a bright bird feeder to fill with seeds and put outside!

WHAT YOU NEED

16×24 LEGO plate

LEGO railing pieces

LEGO basic bricks

10×20 LEGO plate

LEGO decorations (optional)

birdseed

scoop

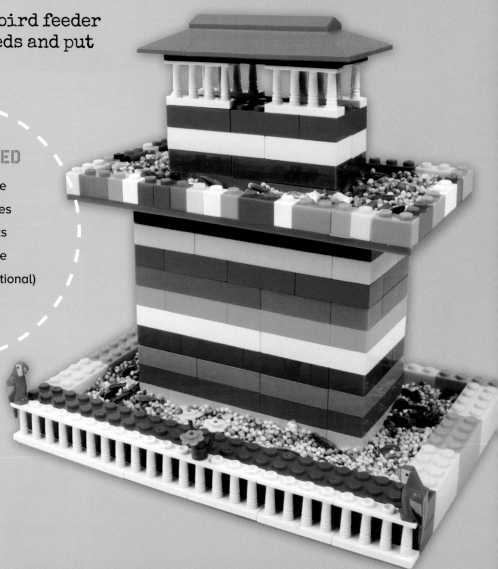

1. Use LEGO railing pieces or basic bricks to form a fence around one long edge of the larger LEGO plate.

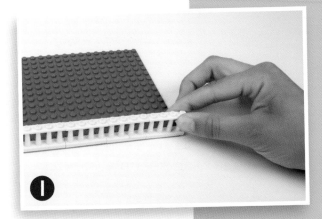

2. Behind the fence, build a wall using basic bricks. Make the wall as high as the fence.

3. Use basic bricks to extend the wall along the two shorter sides of the plate. Leave the last row of **studs** on the other long side of the plate uncovered.

4. Use basic bricks that are one stud wide to make a narrow wall along the other long side of the plate.

Continued on the next page.

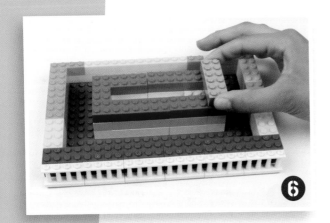

5. In the center of the plate, use basic bricks to make a rectangle that is 6 by 14 **studs**. This is the foundation for the center structure of the feeder.

6 **Stack** several layers of basic bricks on top of the center foundation. Continue until the structure is about 10 or 11 bricks tall.

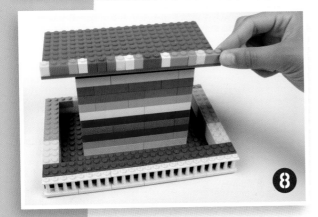

7. Attach the smaller LEGO plate to the top of the center structure. This will be the upper platform.

8 Use 1×1 basic bricks to build a fence around the upper platform.

9 In the center of the upper platform, use basic bricks to build a rectangle. Make the rectangle 4 by 10 studs. This is the foundation for the feeder's upper center structure.

10. **Stack** two or three layers of basic bricks on top of the upper foundation.

11 Decorate the feeder however you like! You can build a roof, add windows, and more.

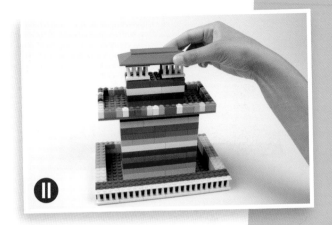

12 Fill the space surrounding the lower and upper center structures with birdseed.

13. Set the bird feeder on a porch, deck, outdoor table, or another spot outside. Watch birds flock to your colorful creation to eat!

K'NEX BRIDGE

Connect, twist, and secure K'NEX pieces to make a cool bridge!

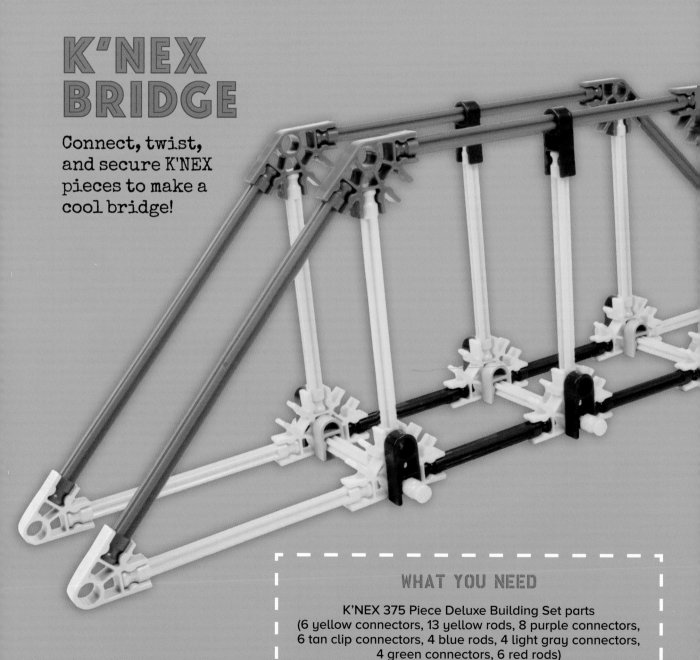

1. Put a yellow connector on each end of a yellow rod.

2. Attach a purple connector to each end of the rod.

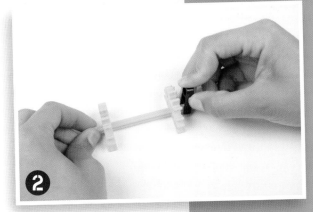

3. Attach a tan clip connector to the rod inside each yellow connector. This completes a crossbeam for the bridge.

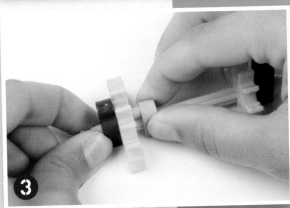

4. Repeat steps 1 through 3 to create two more crossbeams.

5. Set the crossbeams side by side. Connect the crossbeams with blue rods. This completes the bridge deck.

Continued on the next page.

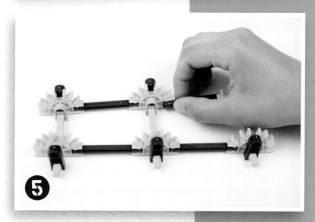

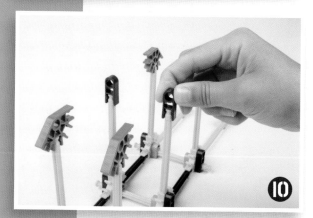

6. Attach a yellow rod to each of the yellow connectors on the ends of the bridge deck. The yellow rods should point away from the blue rods.

7 Attach a light gray connector to the other end of each yellow rod you added in step 6.

8. Attach a yellow rod to the top of each of the six yellow connectors.

9 Attach green connectors to the four yellow rods on the corners of the bridge deck.

10 Attach purple connectors to the yellow rods in the center of the bridge deck.

11 Push a red rod through the hole in a purple connector. Turn the connector so you can attach the ends of the red rod to the green connectors. Repeat on the other side of the bridge with another red rod.

12 Attach a red rod to each of the four light gray connectors. Attach the other end of each rod to a green connector.

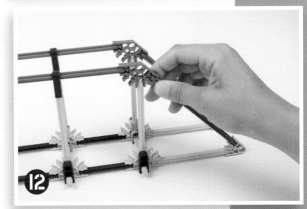

13. Your bridge is complete! Break it apart and try building a bridge using a different design.

CANDY CANE CASTLE

Construct a sturdy, colorful castle that looks like candy!

WHAT YOU NEED

white & red basic LEGO bricks • 32×32 LEGO plate • white & red LEGO column bricks

white LEGO arch brick • white LEGO window • small striped LEGO awning

10×20 LEGO plate • red LEGO plates (1 stud wide) • large & small red LEGO awnings

red LEGO roof pieces • decorative LEGO pieces (LEGO people, trees & more)

1. Use white basic bricks to make a rectangle near one edge of the 32×32 LEGO plate. Make it 12 by 22 **studs**. This rectangle is the building's foundation.

2. The wall of the foundation near the center of the plate will be the front of the castle. Place two column bricks on the front wall. Space them six studs apart.

3. Add an arch brick on top of the columns. This creates the castle's doorway.

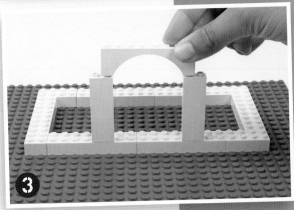

4. Add three layers of basic bricks on the foundation. Alternate between red and white layers. Do not put bricks in the doorway.

Continued on the next page.

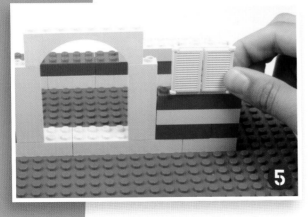

5 Put a LEGO window on the wall next to the doorway.

6 Put a red column brick on each side of the window.

7. Stick a small striped **awning** piece above the window.

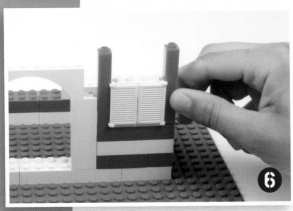

8. Use basic bricks to fill in the space above the window. Fill in the space between the window and door so the tops of each are level.

9. Continue to add alternating white and red layers to make a candy cane pattern. Stop when the walls are even all the way around.

10 Press the 10×20 LEGO plate on top of the castle.

11. Place red LEGO plates that are one **stud** wide around the edges of the 10×20 LEGO plate.

12. Add a layer of white basic bricks around the edge of the building.

13 Add a large red **awning** over the doorway. Outline the roof's edge with red roof pieces.

14. Fill in the rest of the roof with red basic bricks. Use basic bricks, a small red awning piece, and roof pieces to form a tower on the roof.

15 Add decorations to your castle! Build a walkway or a garden. Use LEGO trees, round LEGO pieces, and more!

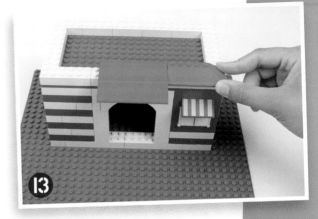

 **TIP** If you don't have LEGO decorations, get creative! Find other materials to complete your project.

PULLEY ELEVATOR

Build a working elevator with just LEGOs and string!

WHAT YOU NEED

LEGO basic bricks

16×32 LEGO plate · LEGO window

LEGO pulley · LEGO axle plate

6×12 LEGO plate · LEGO person

string · scissors

LEGO decorations (optional)

1. Use basic bricks to outline a rectangle on one end of the 16×32 LEGO plate. Make the rectangle 10 by 16 **studs**.

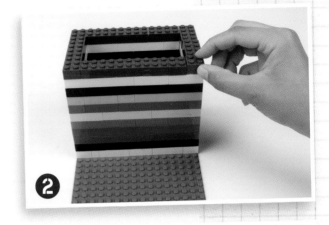

2 **Stack** more layers of basic bricks on top of the rectangle. Continue until the structure is about 19 bricks tall.

3. Place a LEGO window on the side of the wall.

4 Attach a **pulley** to a LEGO **axle** plate.

5 Add more basic brick layers until the walls are even with the top of the window. Before completing the top layer, attach the pulley and axle plate to the top of the structure. Make sure the pulley sticks out from the wall's outer edge.

6. Complete the layer of bricks so the walls are even with the top of the window all the way around. Then add one final layer.

Continued on the next page.

7. Use basic bricks to build a wall around the edges of the 6×12 LEGO plate. Make the wall about five bricks tall. This is the elevator car.

8 Attach a 1×6 brick across the middle of the elevator car. Add a LEGO person on top of the car.

9 Cut a long piece of string. Tie one end around the narrow brick on top of the elevator car.

10 Wrap the string over the **pulley**. Pull on the string and watch your elevator car rise!

11. Add LEGO decorations to the plate, building, or elevator car.

WRECKING BALL

Build a rubber-band wrecking ball that can topple LEGO towers!

27

1. Lay the box down. Stand the paper towel tube up 2 inches (5 cm) in from one short side of the box. Center the tube along that side. Trace around the tube. Carefully use a craft knife to cut the circle out.

2. Cover your work surface with newspaper. Paint the box and paper towel tube. Let the paint dry.

3. Decorate the box and paper towel tube with black electrical tape.

4. Make four evenly spaced cuts in one end of the paper towel tube. Each cut should be 1½ inches (4 cm) long. This creates four tabs.

5. Push the end of the tube with the tabs through the hole in the box. Fold the tabs against the inside of the box. Tape them in place.

6. Stand the box up so the tube is at the top. Poke a nail vertically through the tube.

7. Put rocks or other heavy objects in the box. Tape the box closed.

8 Wrap rubber bands around the bouncy ball until it is completely covered. This is the wrecking ball.

9. Cut a long piece of string. Thread one end through the holes you made in the paper towel tube. Tie a large knot in the end of the string. Make sure the knot won't fit through the holes.

10 Thread the other end of the string under a couple of the rubber bands on the ball. Pull the string until the ball hangs about 2 inches (5 cm) from the ground. Tie a knot to hold the ball in place.

11 Build LEGO towers of different widths and heights. Set them up in front of the wrecking ball. Pull the ball back. Let go of the ball so it swings toward the LEGO towers. What happens?

MAKERSPACE MAINTENANCE

Being a maker is not just about the finished craft. It's about communicating and **collaborating** with others as you create. The best makers also learn from their creations. They think of ways to improve them next time.

CLEANING UP

When you're done with a project, be sure to tidy up your area. Put away tools and supplies. Make sure they are organized so others can find them easily.

SAFE STORAGE

Sometimes you won't finish a project in one makerspace **session**. That's OK! Just find a safe place to store your project until you can work on it again.

MAKER FOR LIFE!

Maker project possibilities are endless. Get inspired by the materials in your makerspace. Invite new makers to your space. Check out what other makers are creating. Never stop making!

GLOSSARY

accurate – free from error.

awning – a rooflike cover extending over or in front of a place, creating shelter.

axle – a bar that connects two wheels.

collaborate – to work with another person or group in order to do something or reach a goal.

online – connected to the Internet.

permission – when a person in charge says it's okay to do something.

pulley – a wheel over which a rope or cable may be pulled. It helps move or change the direction of heavy loads.

session – a period of time used for a specific purpose or activity.

stack – to arrange things neatly in a pile or layer.

stud – a small, button-like piece projecting from a surface.

ONLINE RESOURCES

Booklinks
NONFICTION
NETWORK
FREE! ONLINE NONFICTION RESOURCES

To learn more about architecture projects, visit **abdobooklinks.com**. These links are routinely monitored and updated to provide the most current information available.

INDEX